for YOU—
my plant-loving
friend

Tom Wilson

First published in Great Britain in 1982 by
Exley Publications Ltd, 12 Ye Corner,
Chalk Hill, Watford, Herts WD1 4BS
Printed in Hungary by Kossuth Printing House

British Library Cataloguing in Publication Data
Wilson, Tom, *19---*
    Plants are some of my favourite people: Ziggy.
    1. Wit and humour, Pictorial
    I. Title
    741.5'973   NC1429.W5793
    ISBN 0-905521-68-4

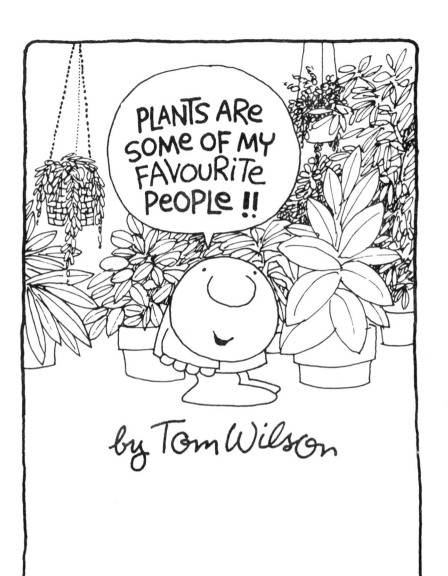

by Tom Wilson

EXLEY

Tom Wilson

YOU CAN COMPLAIN
BECAUSE ROSES HAVE THORNS,
OR
YOU CAN BE GRATEFUL
BECAUSE THORN BUSHES
HAVE ROSES

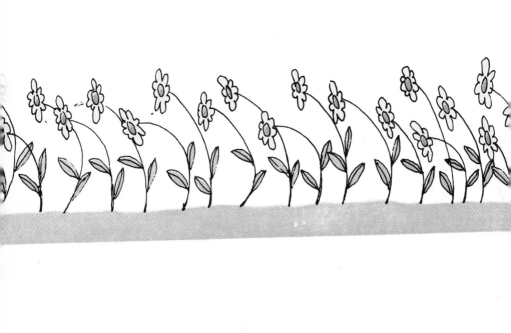

IF THE GRASS LOOKS GREENER IN THE OTHER FELLOW'S GARDEN ...IT'S USUALLY BECAUSE HE'S USING A BETTER BRAND OF FERTILIZER...

Tom Wilson

..FLOWERS HELP TO MAKE UP FOR
ALL THE UGLY IN THE WORLD !!

4

5

Other gift books from Exley Publications

Ziggy: Pets Are Friends Who Share Your Rainy Days £2.95. This is another popular cartoon book about Ziggy. Ziggy is a born loser and his endearing failures make him popular with people of all ages. Ziggy's pets are very special little people who run his life for him. Anyone who has loved a pet will see themselves in this book.

Ziggy: Know How Much I Love You £1.95. This must be one of the smallest 'books' on sale: just $2\frac{1}{4}$ x $2\frac{1}{4}$ x 1 inch; yet the surprise concertina fold-out message extends to nearly five feet in length. Packed in a pretty heart-covered slip case this is a magic, zany little book that says it all. Children, mums, dads, lovers, grandads – everyone would love it on a special occasion.

Shopping By Post For Gardeners £3.95 Here at last you can find who supplies unusual plants or equipment – and get them delivered to your door from anywhere in Britain. A super gift for the keen gardener.

Love, A Celebration £5.50 Writers and poets old and new have captured the feeling of being in love in this very personal collection. Gift-wrapped with sealing wax. Give it to someone special.

The Crazy World Of Skiing £3.95 Over 100 hilarious skiing cartoons covering almost every possible and impossible experience on the slopes. The ideal gift book for Christmas for those with broken bones, or a glint of fanaticism in their eyes.

Grandmas and Grandpas, £3.95 Children are close to grandparents, and this reflects that warmth. 'A Grandma is old on the outside and young on the inside.' An endearing book for grand-parents.

To Dad, £3.95 'Fathers are always right, and even if they're not right, they're never actually wrong.' Dads will love this book – it's so true to life! A regular favourite.

To Mum, £3.95 'When I'm sad she patches me up with laughter.' A thoughtful, joyous gift for mum, entirely created by children. Get it for Mother's Day or her birthday.

Simply order through your bookshop, or by post from Exley Publications Ltd, Dept ZPL, 12 Ye Corner, Chalk Hill, Watford, Herts, WD1 4BS. Please add 15p in the £ as a contribution to postage and packing.